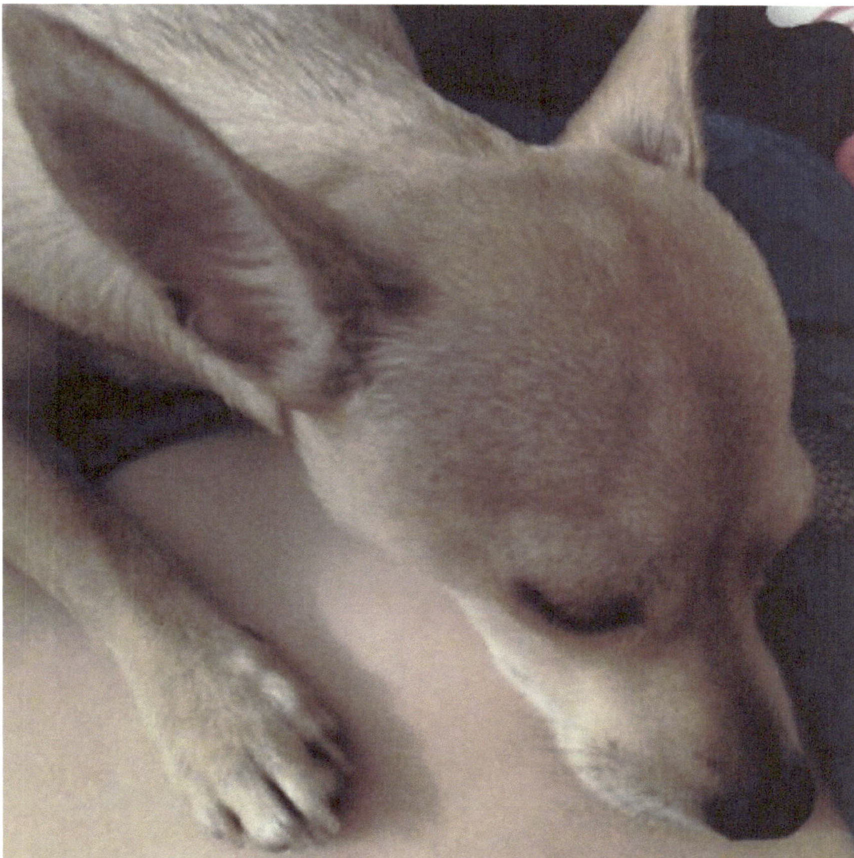

My sweet baby, Collette

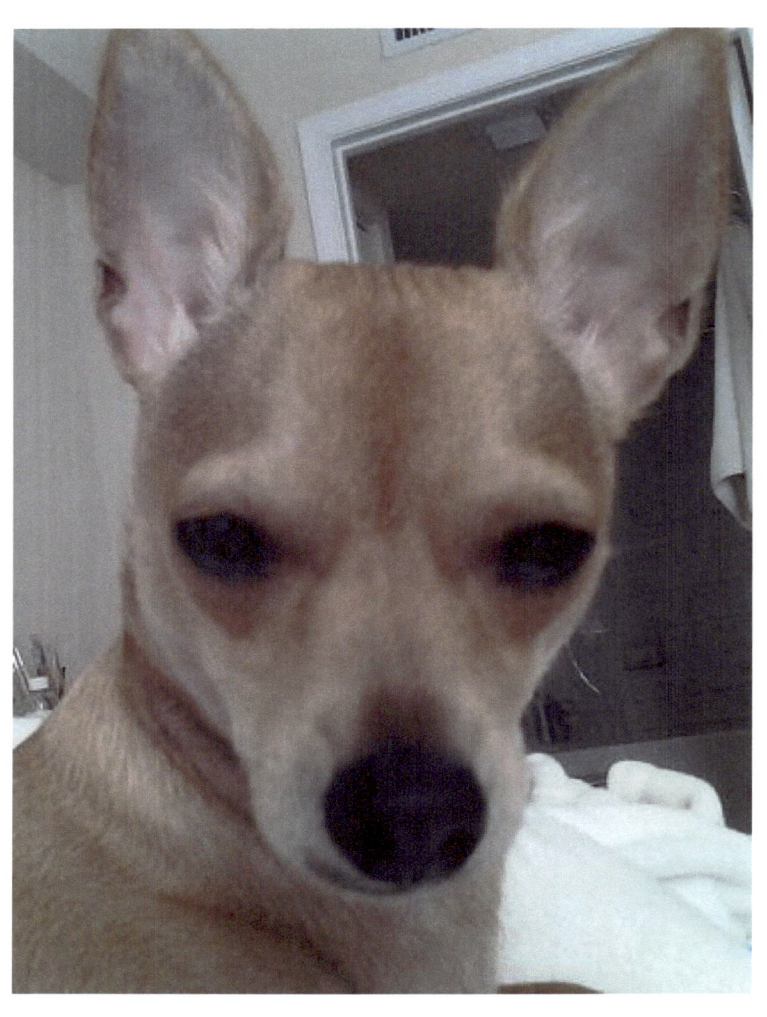

She looks like a deer, thinking...

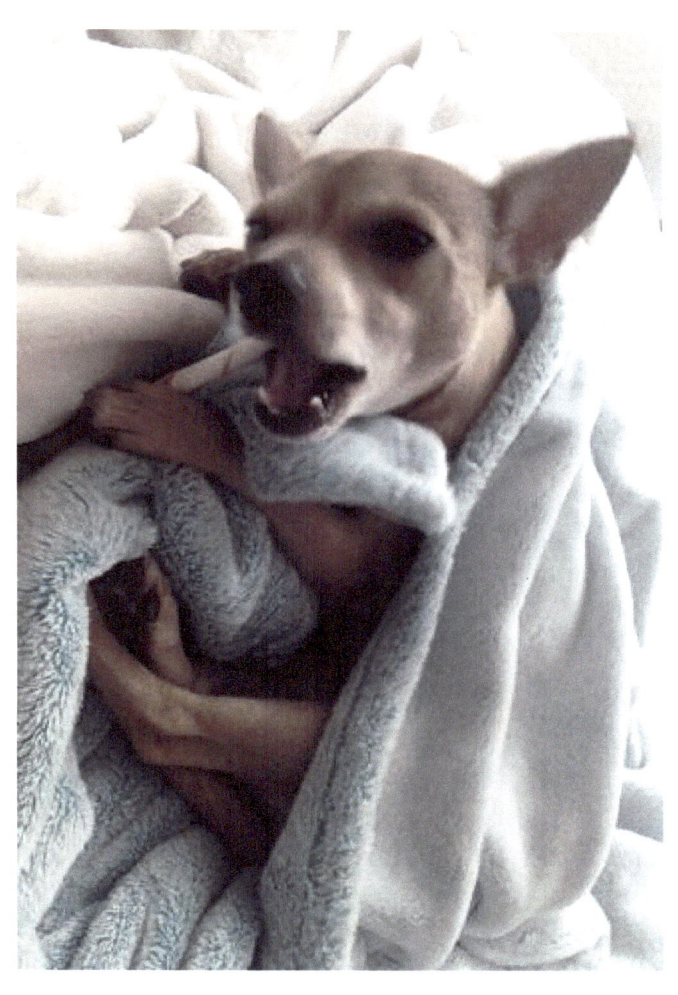

She loves the dingos

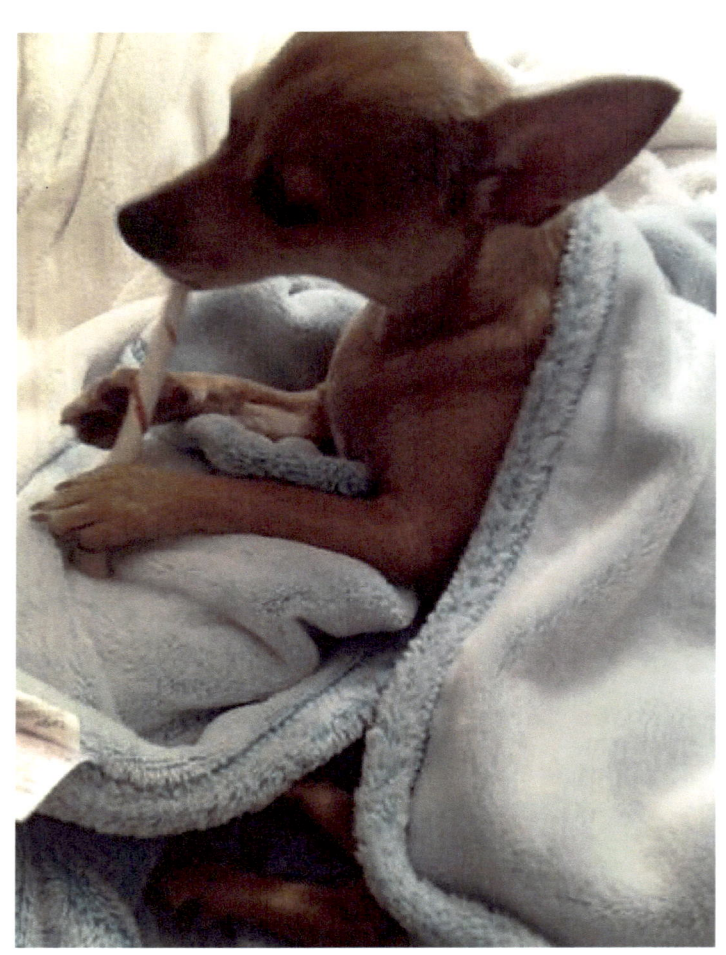

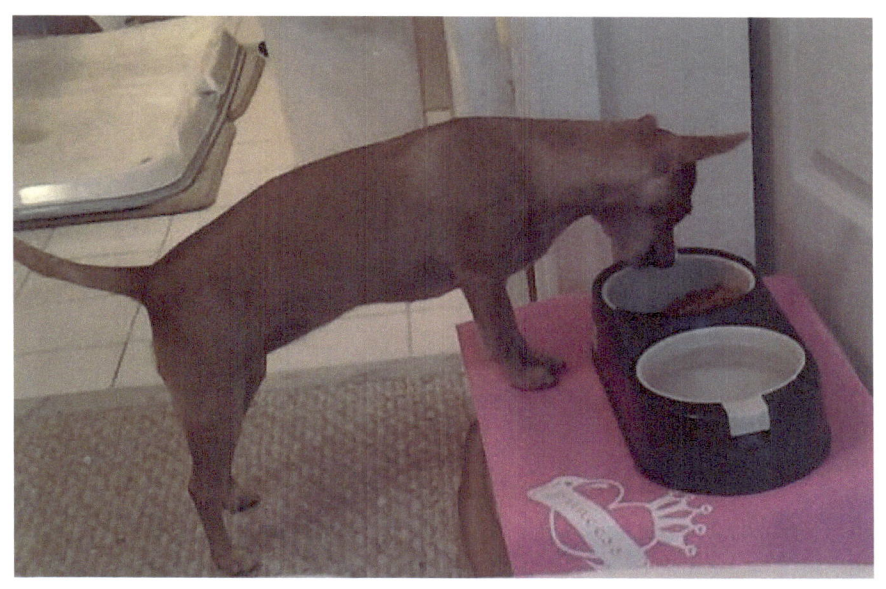

Princess Collette, eating

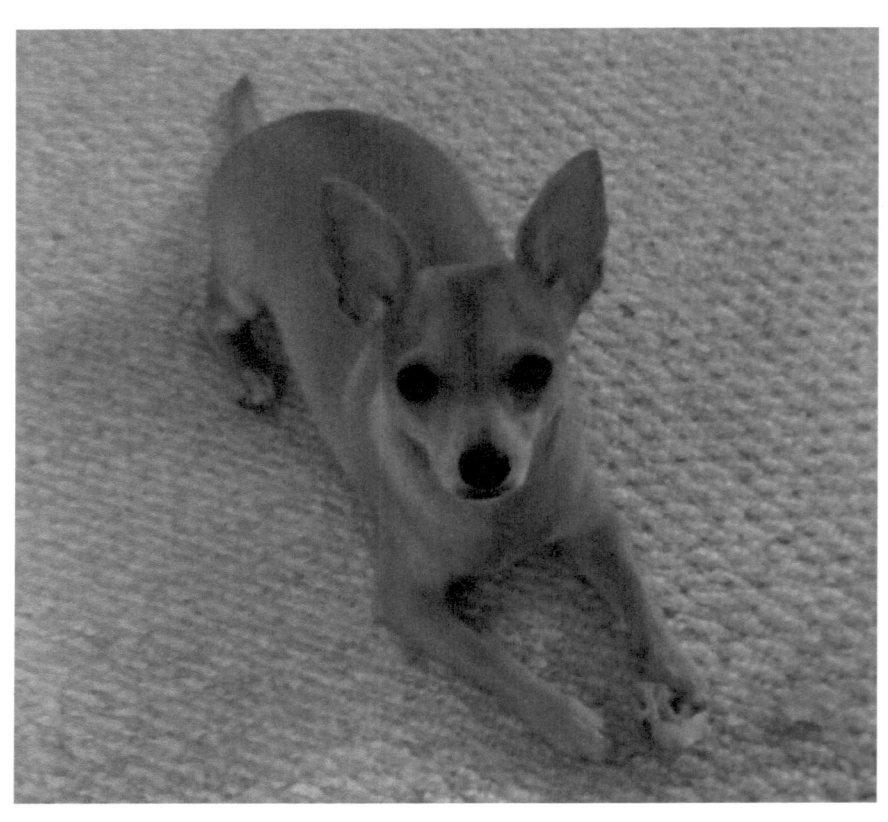

Her classic pose

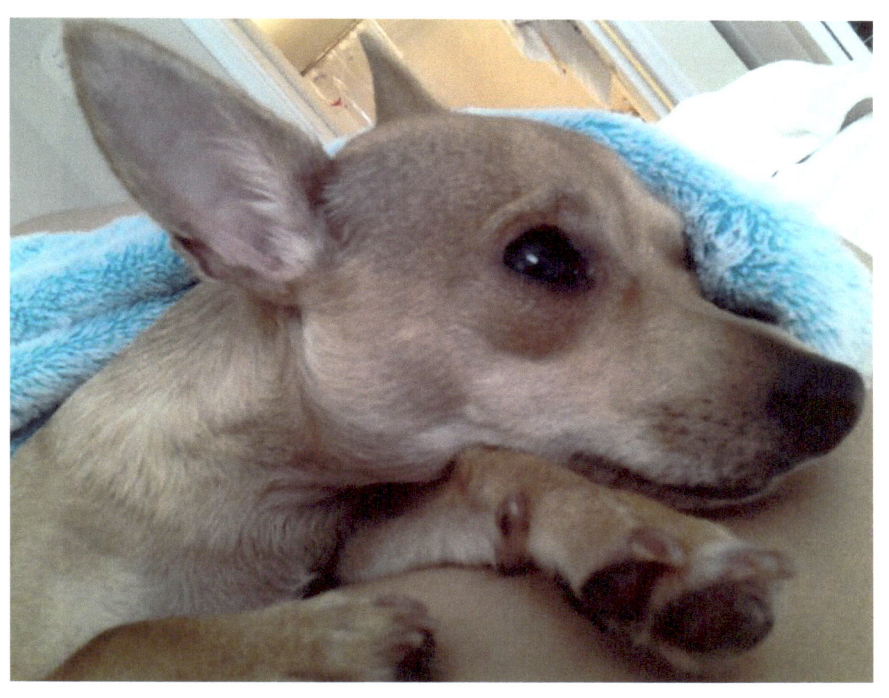

Watching hulu, with me

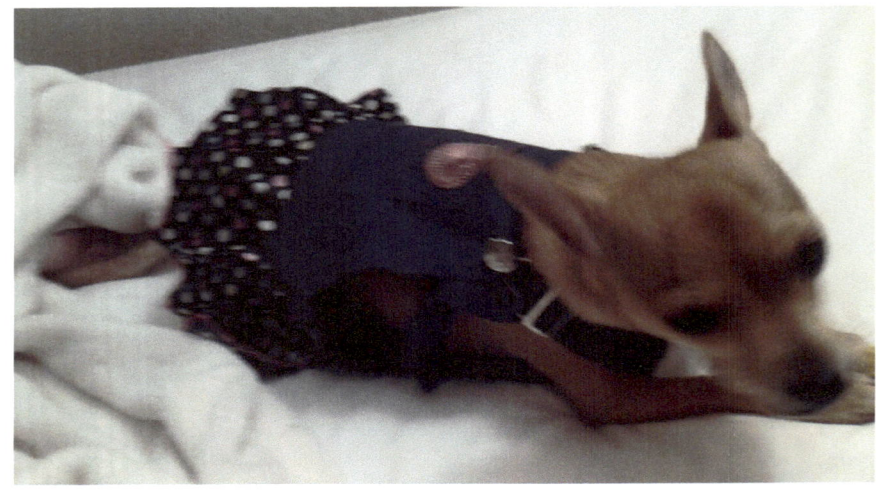

Cute little dress

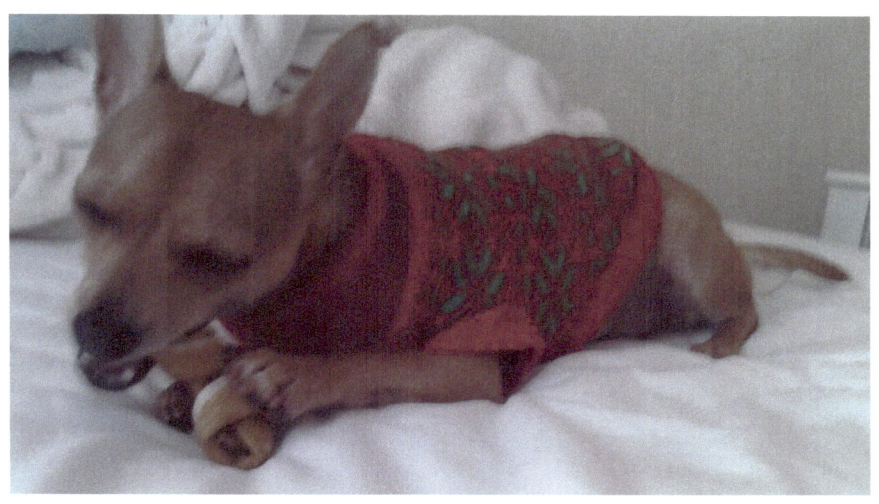

Munching away, enjoying her Christmas sweater

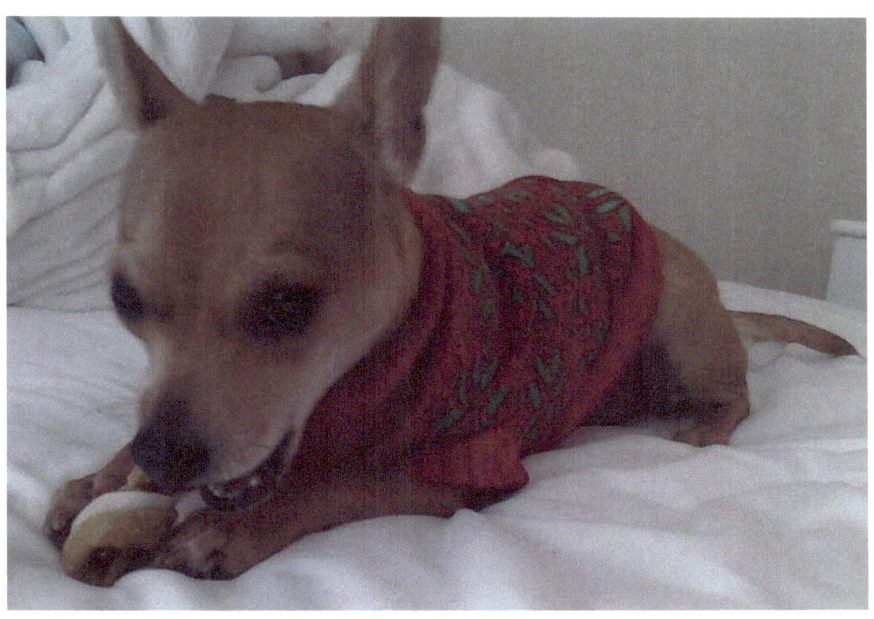

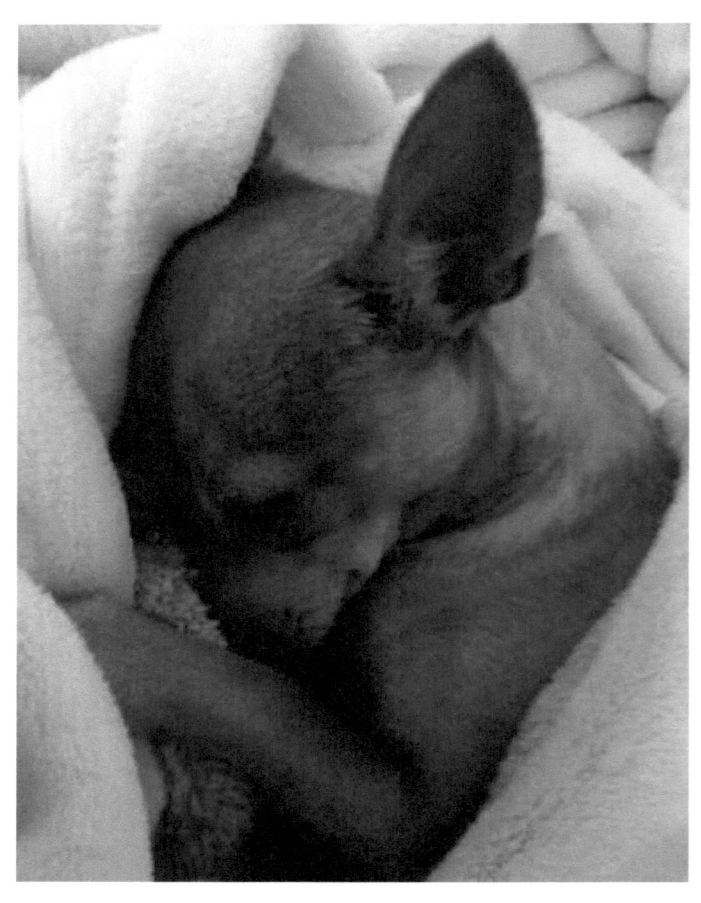

Sleeping Beauty

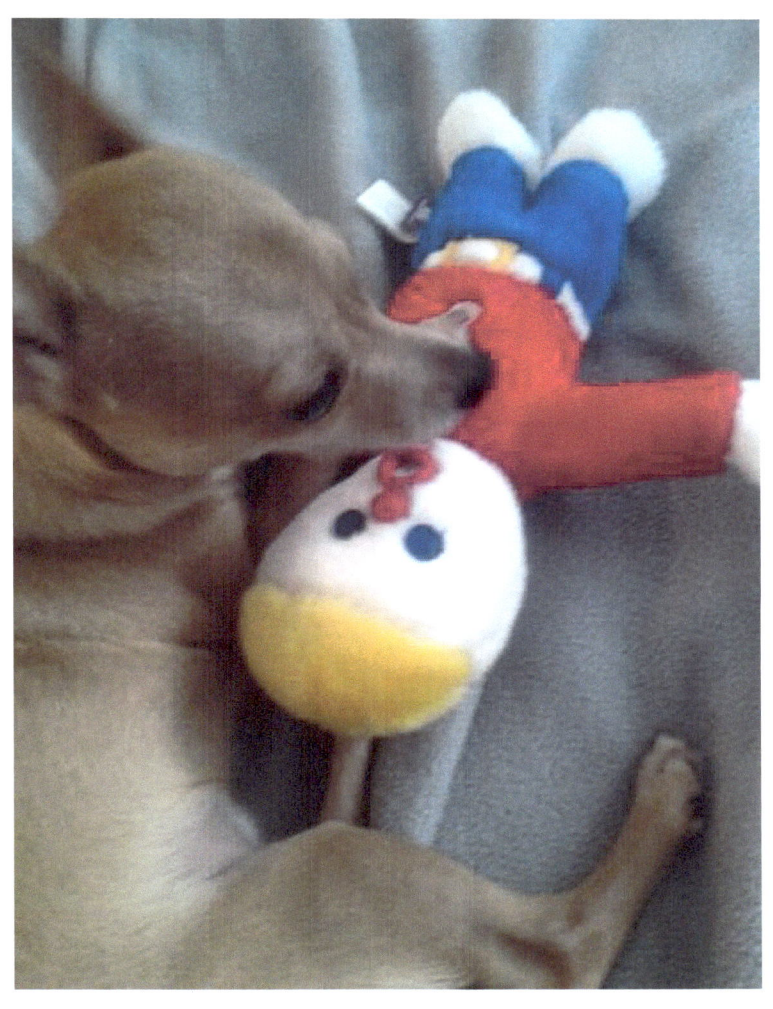

Playing with her Christmas gift

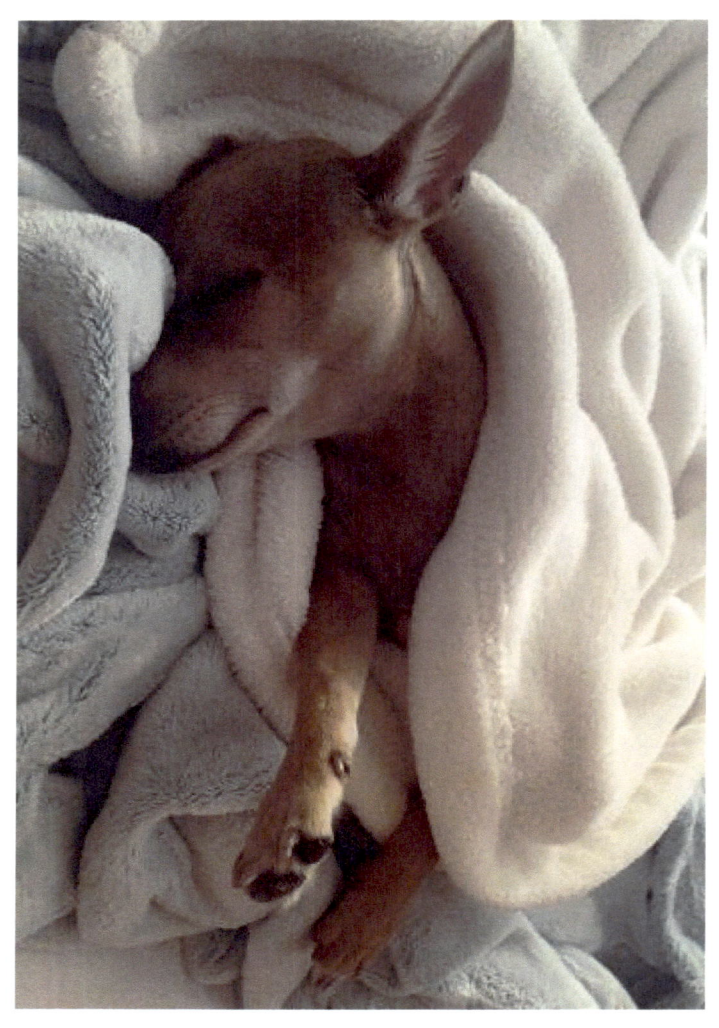

In deep slumber

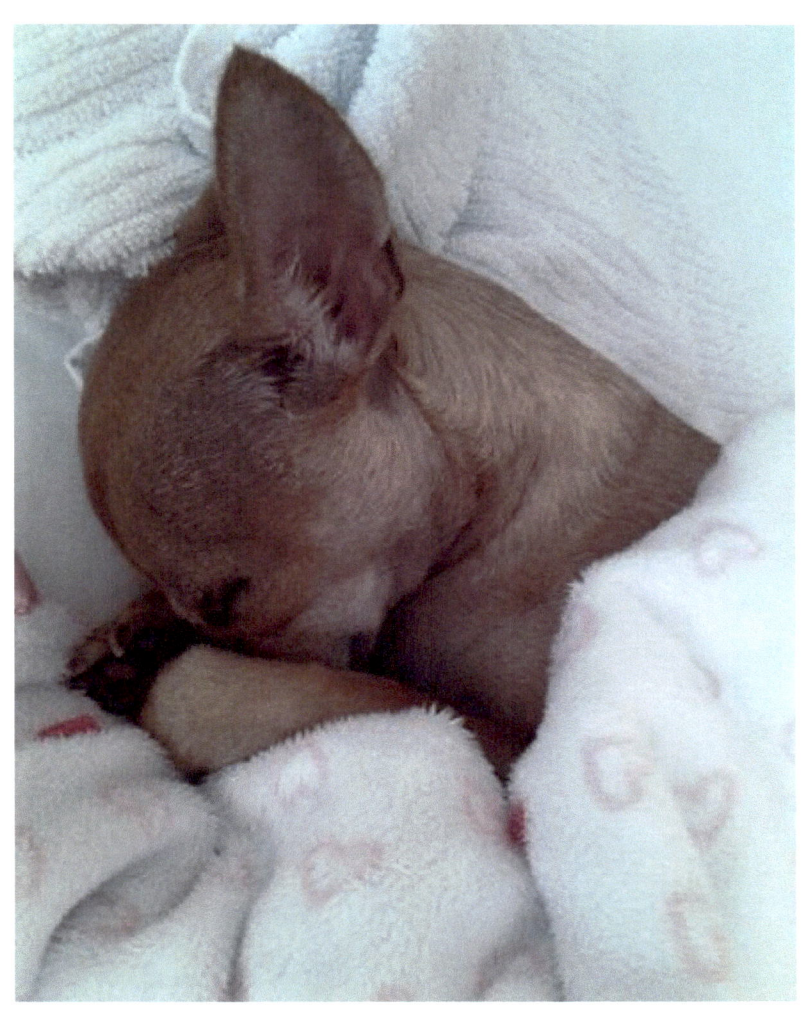

Peek-a-boo

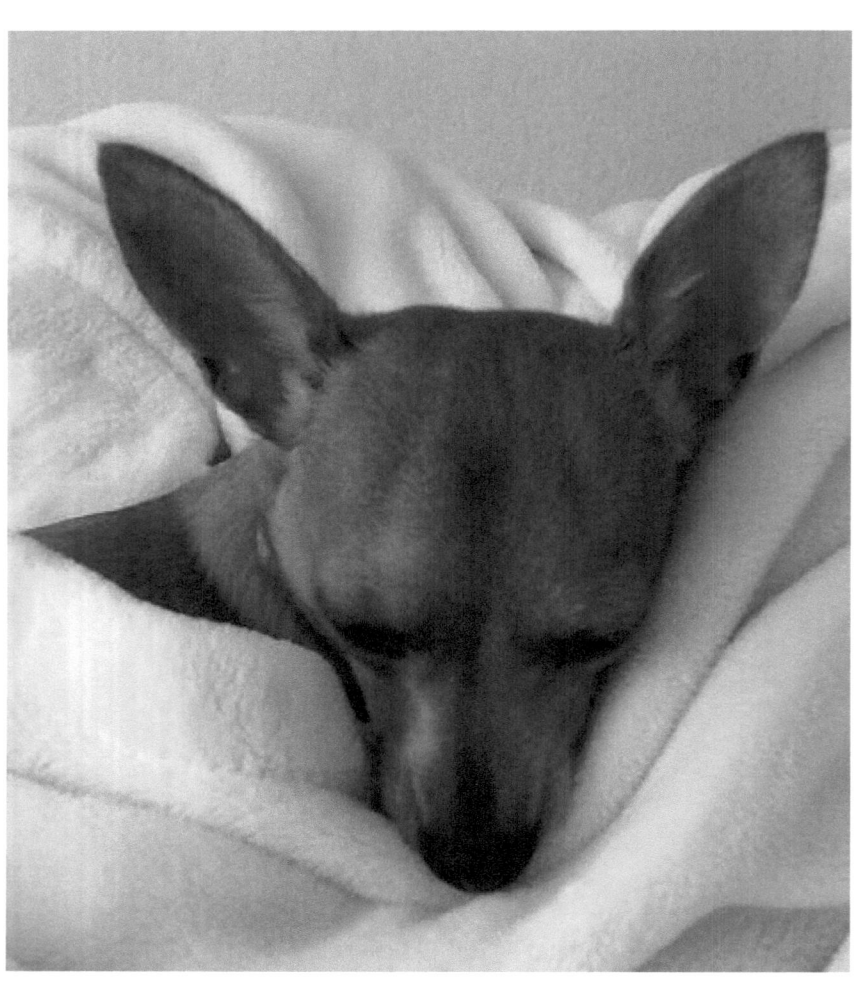

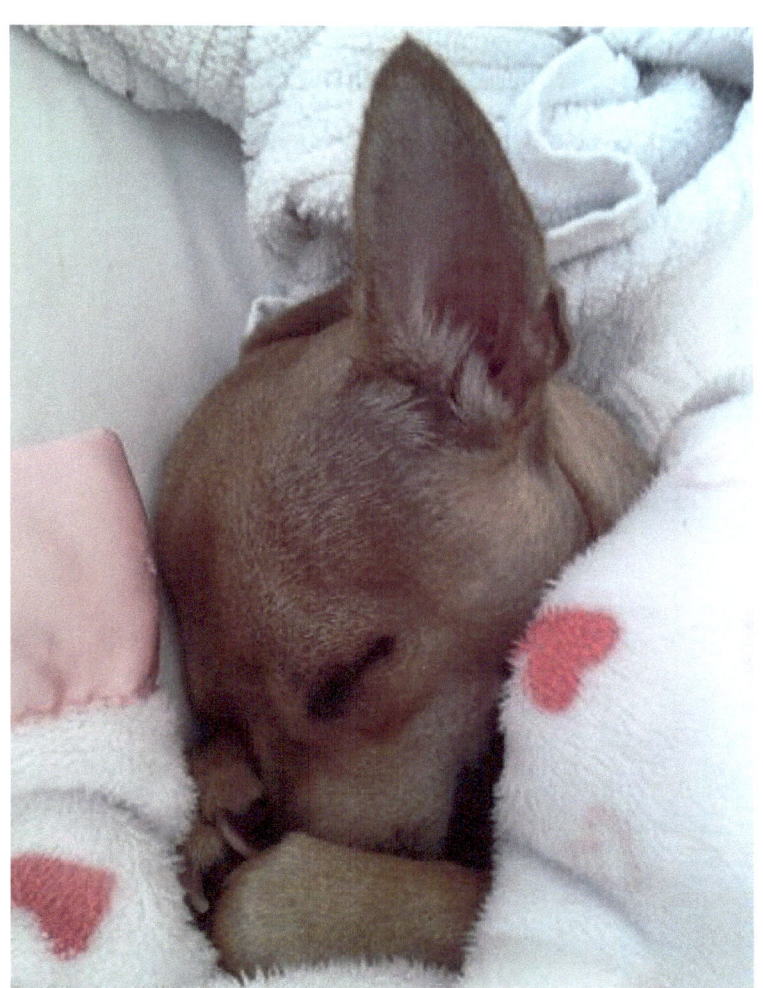

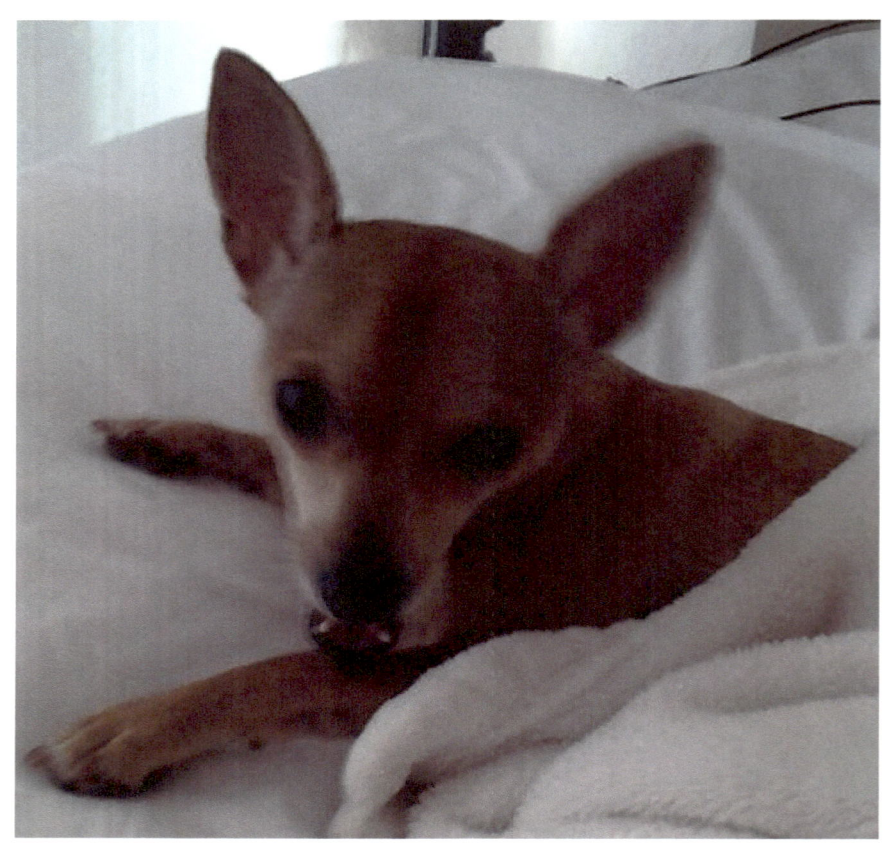

Chewing on her rawhide bone

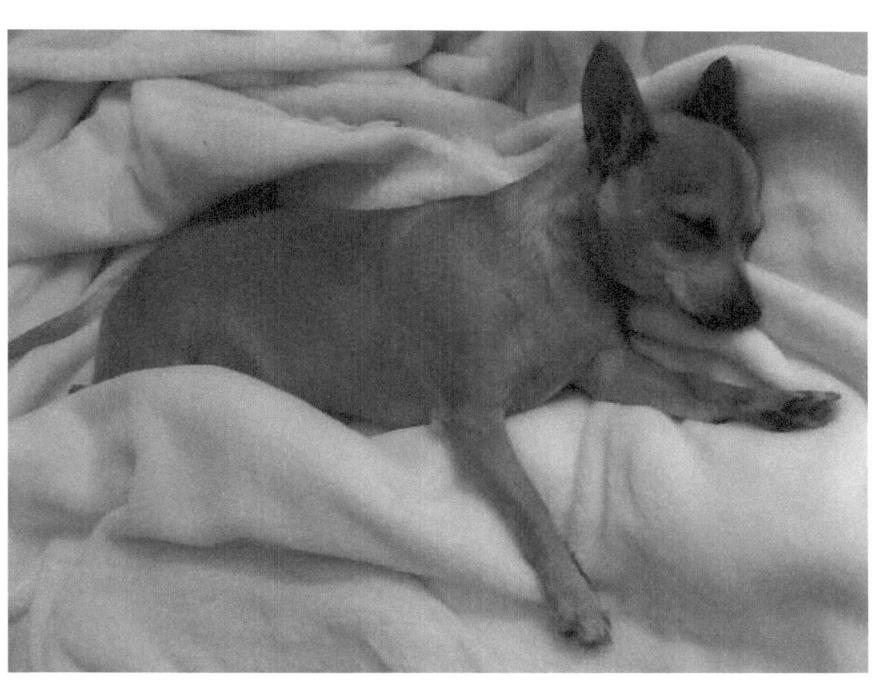

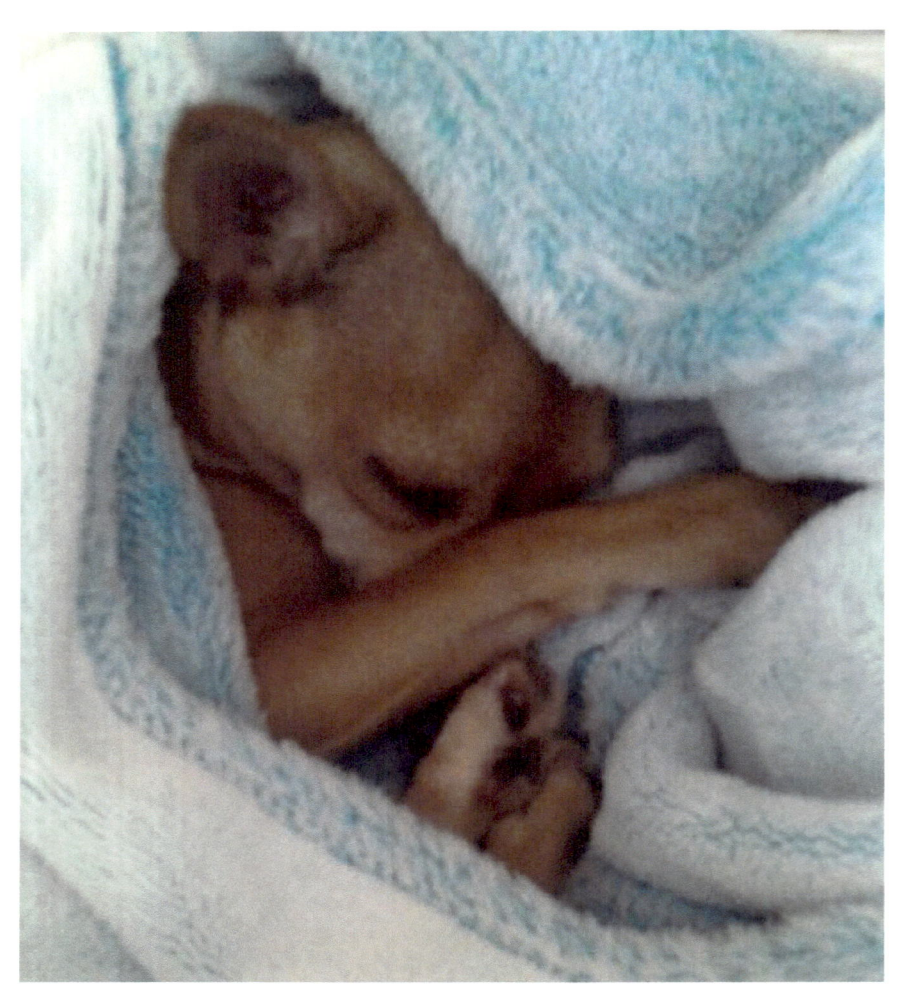

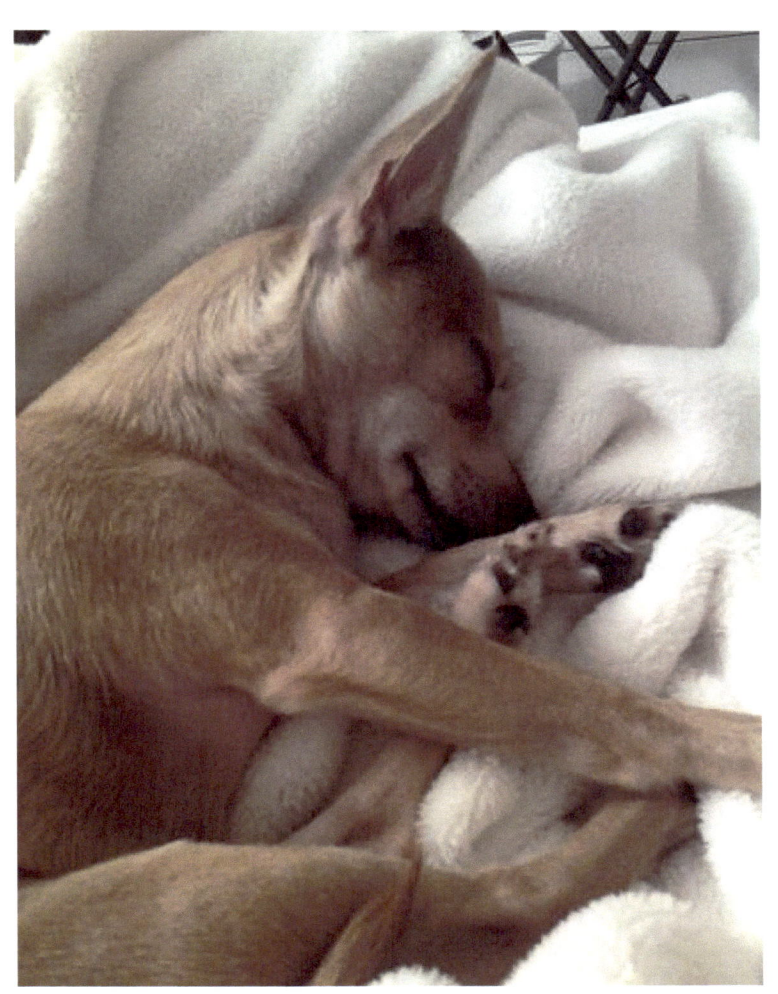

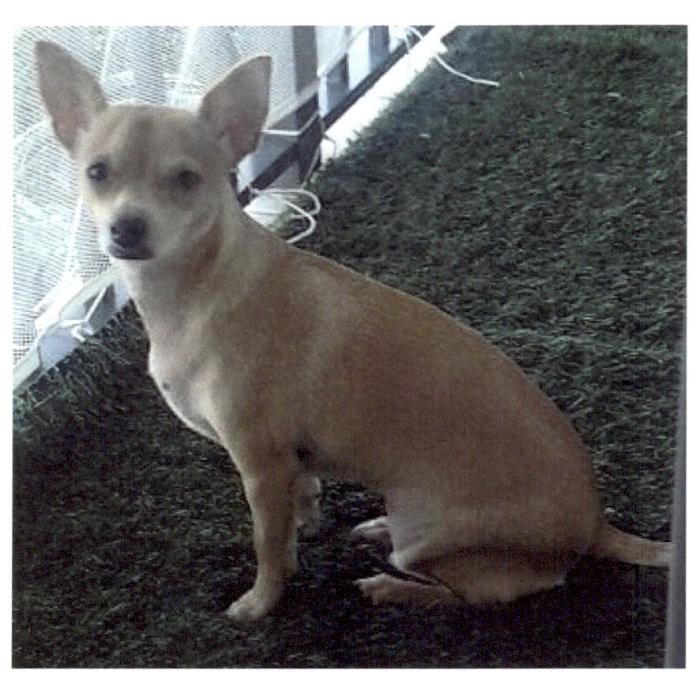

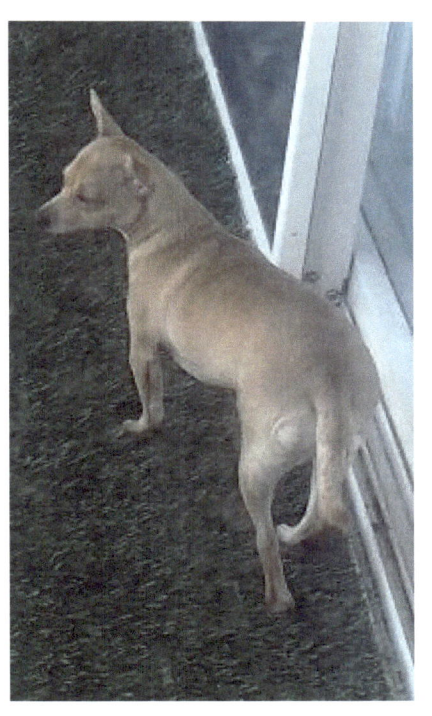

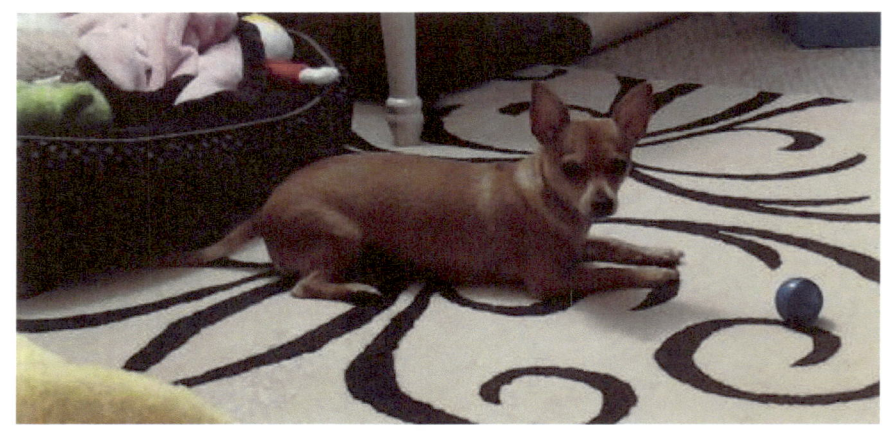

Her play areas

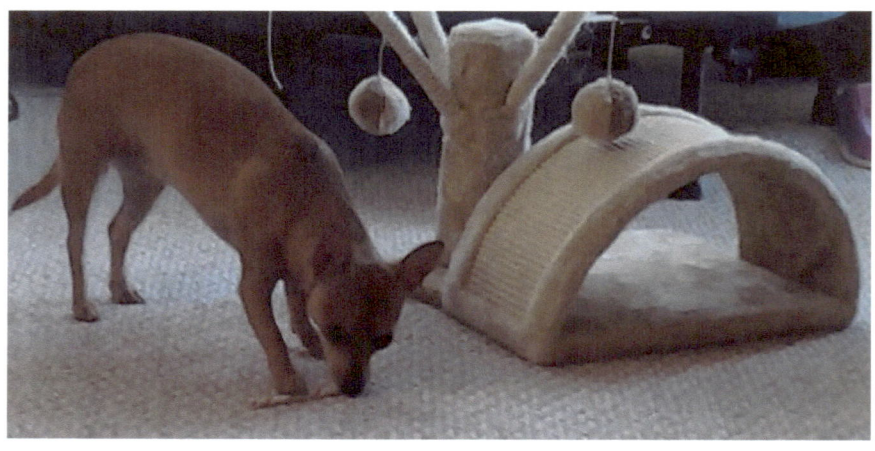

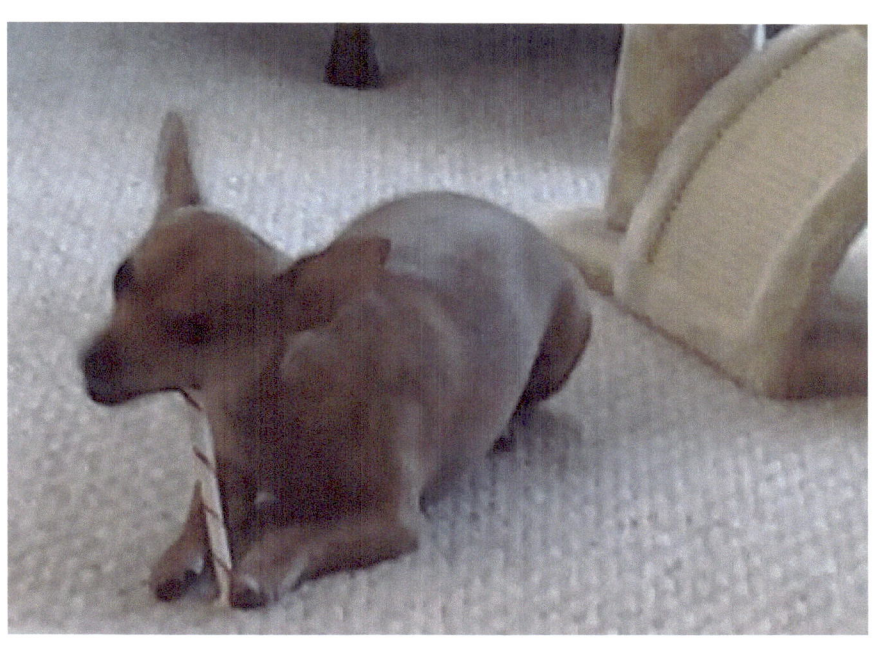

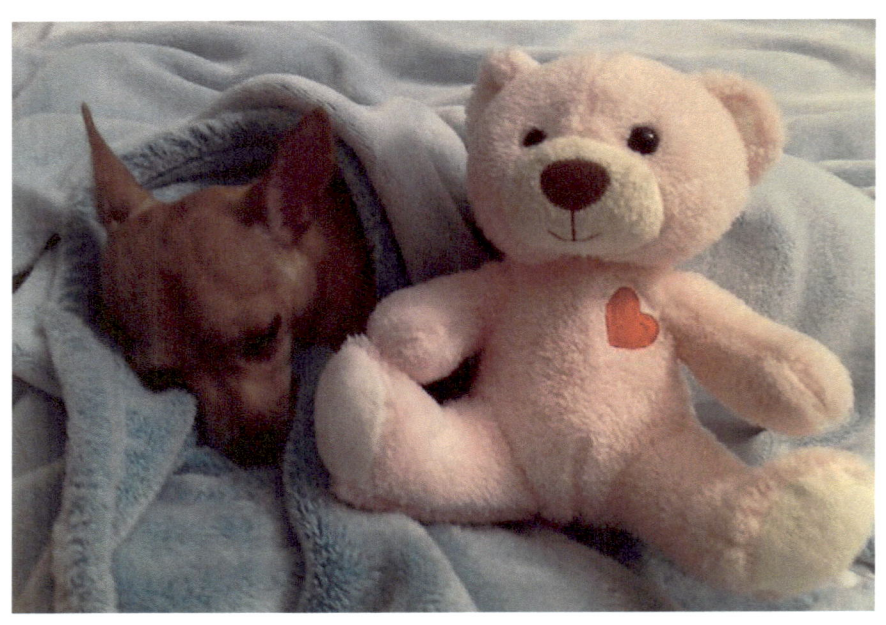

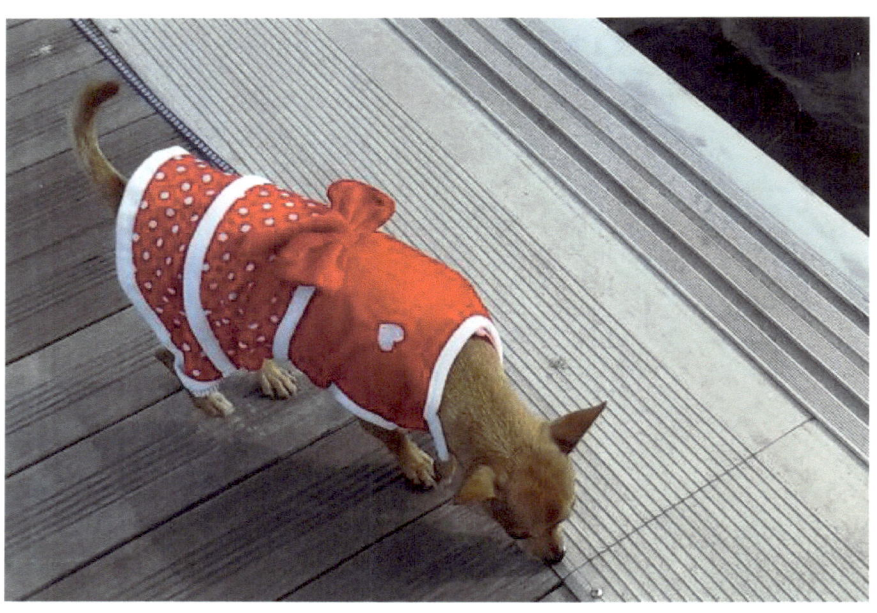

Happy to be outdoors

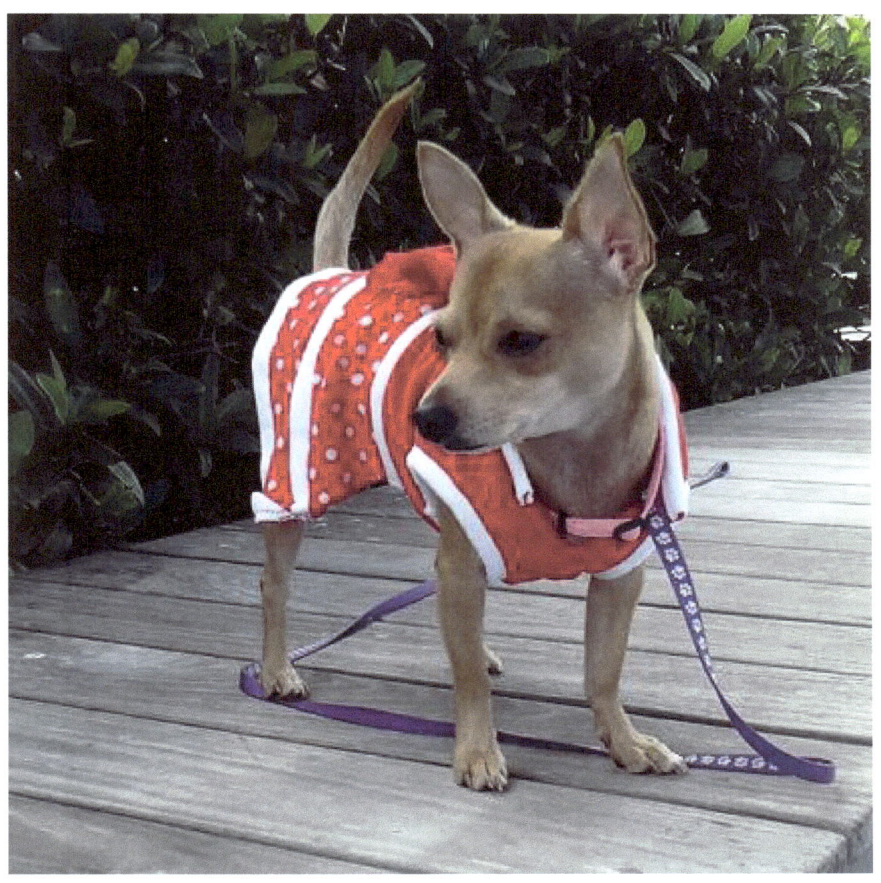

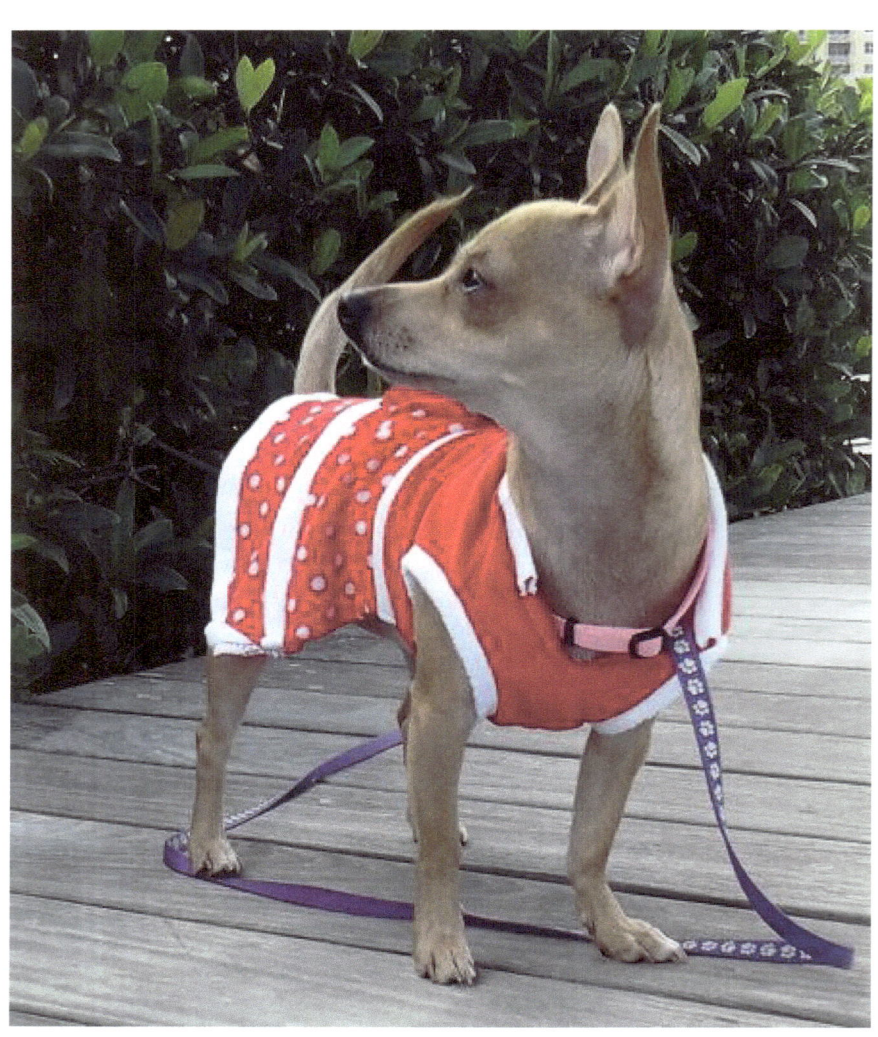

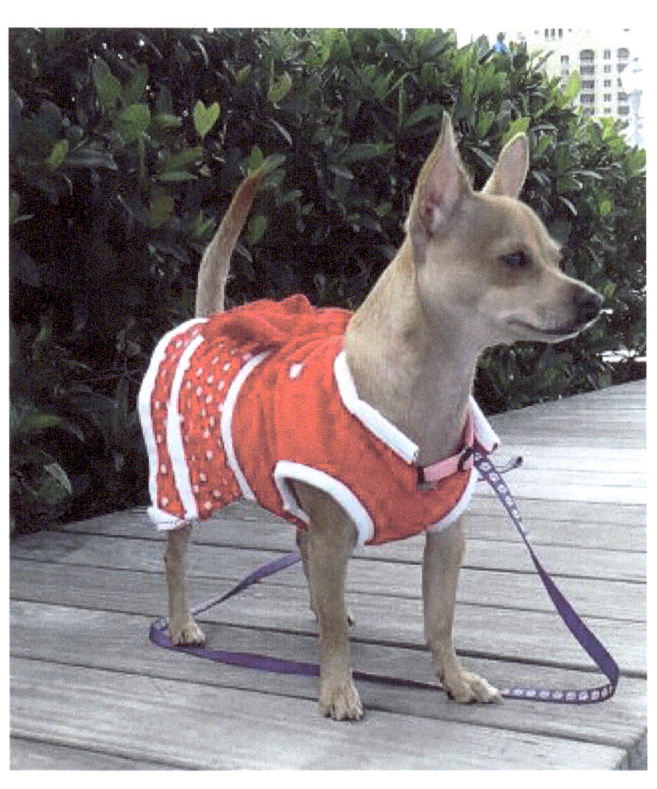

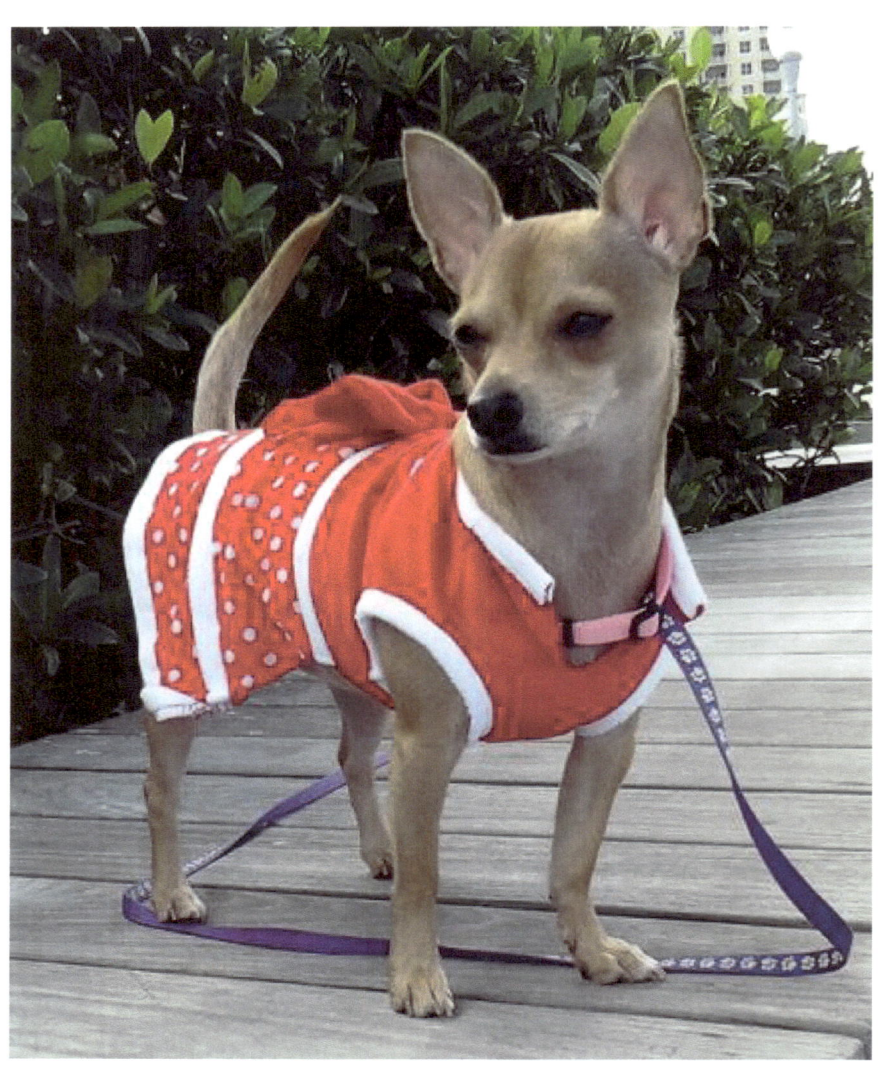

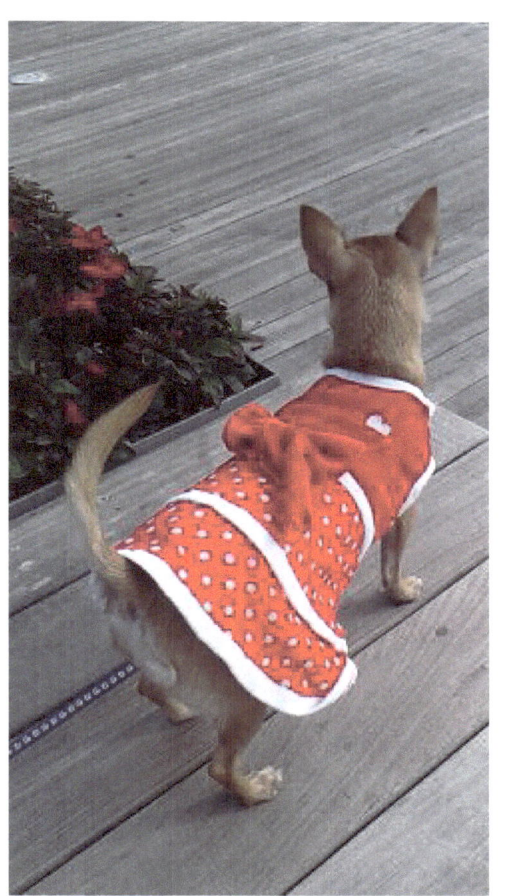

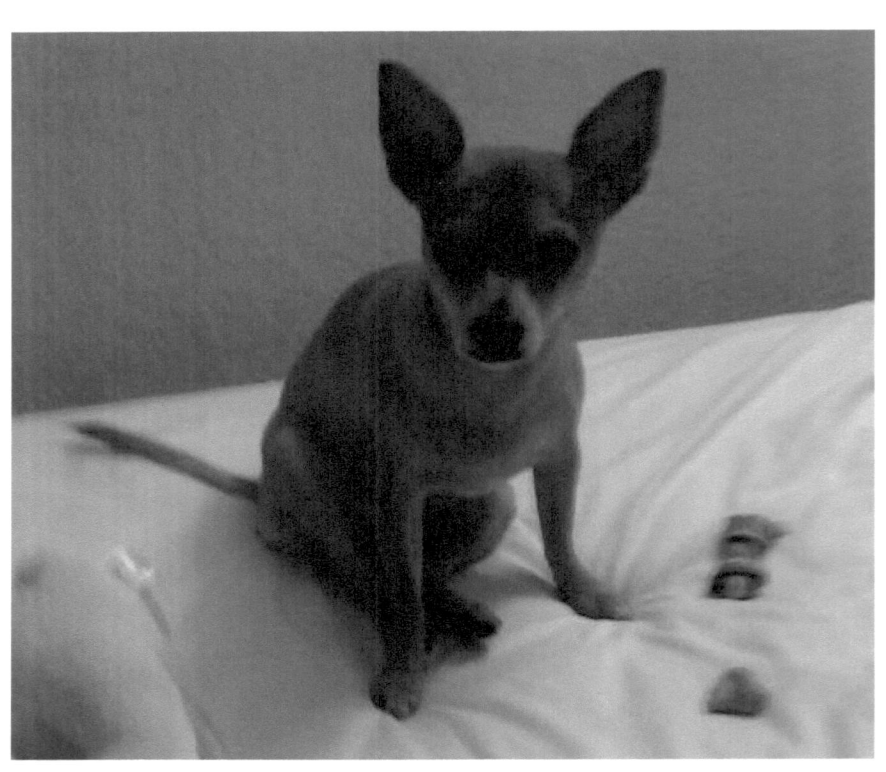

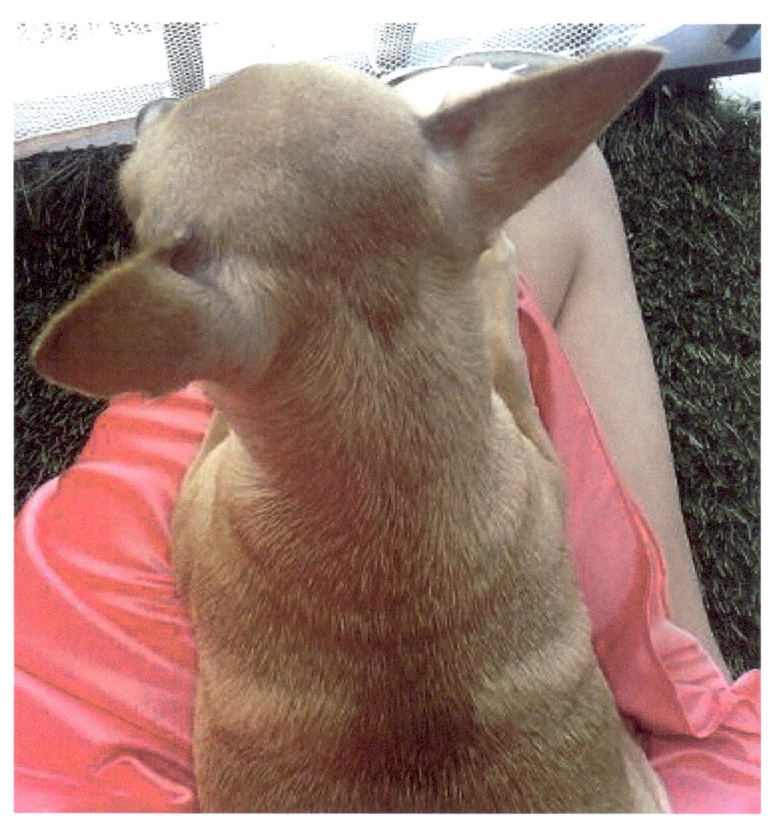

Enjoying the view

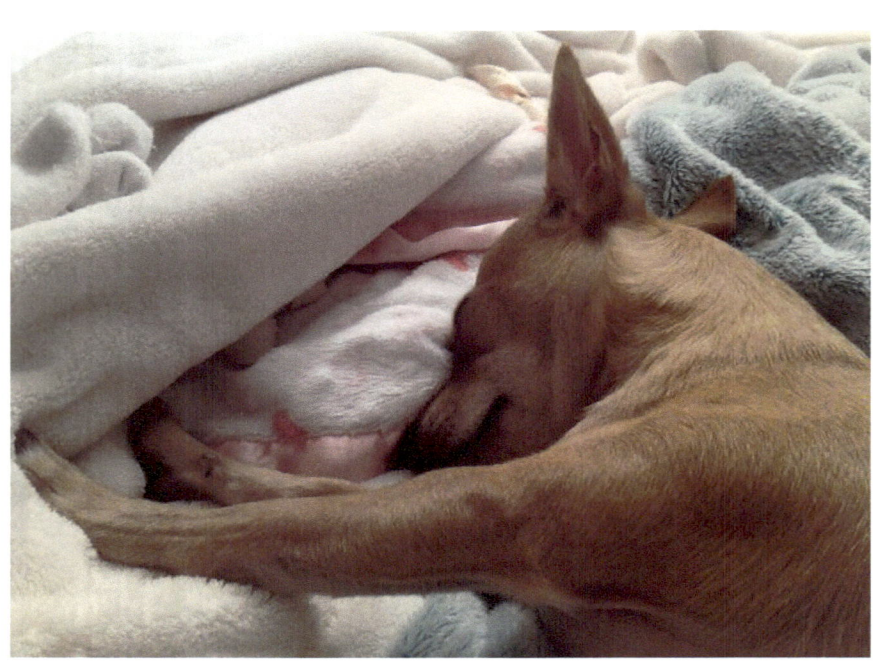

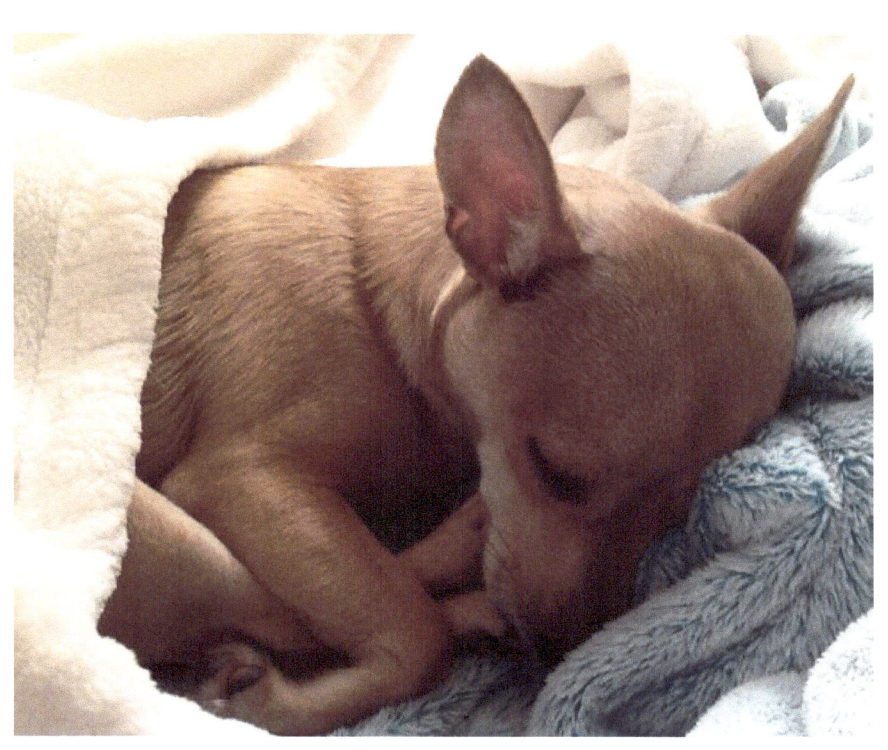

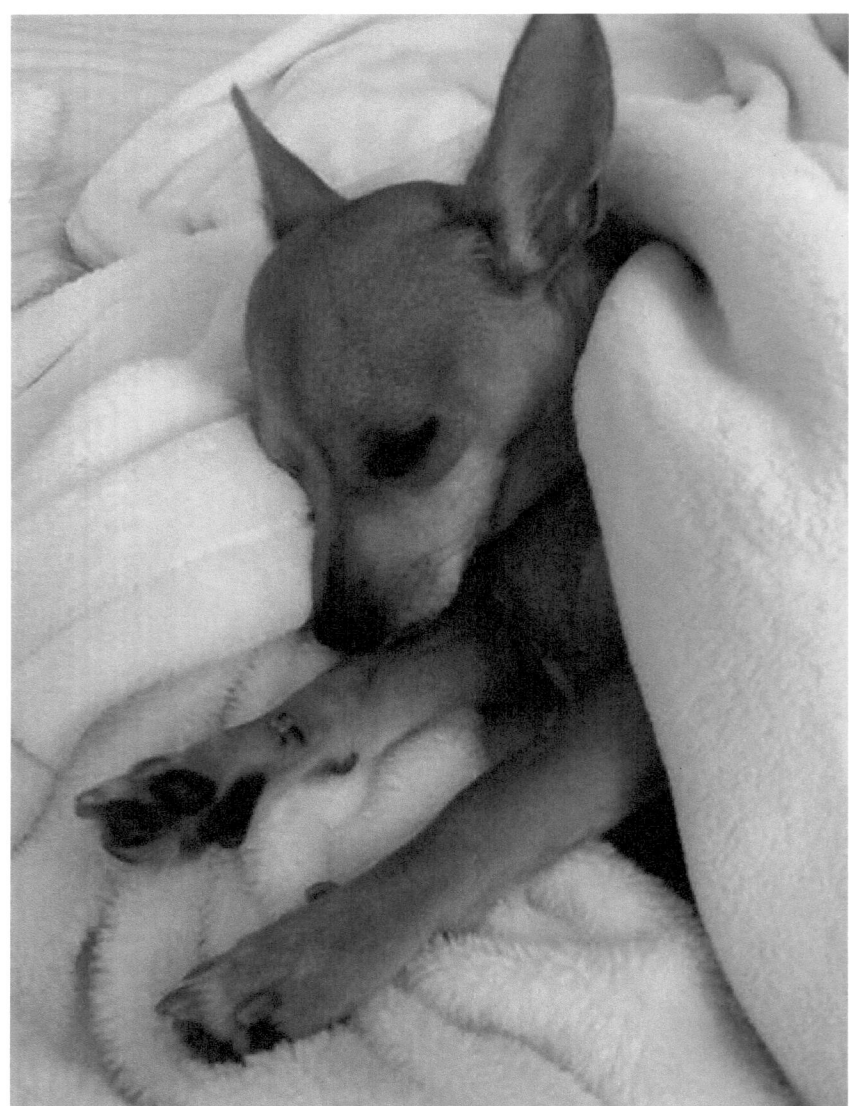

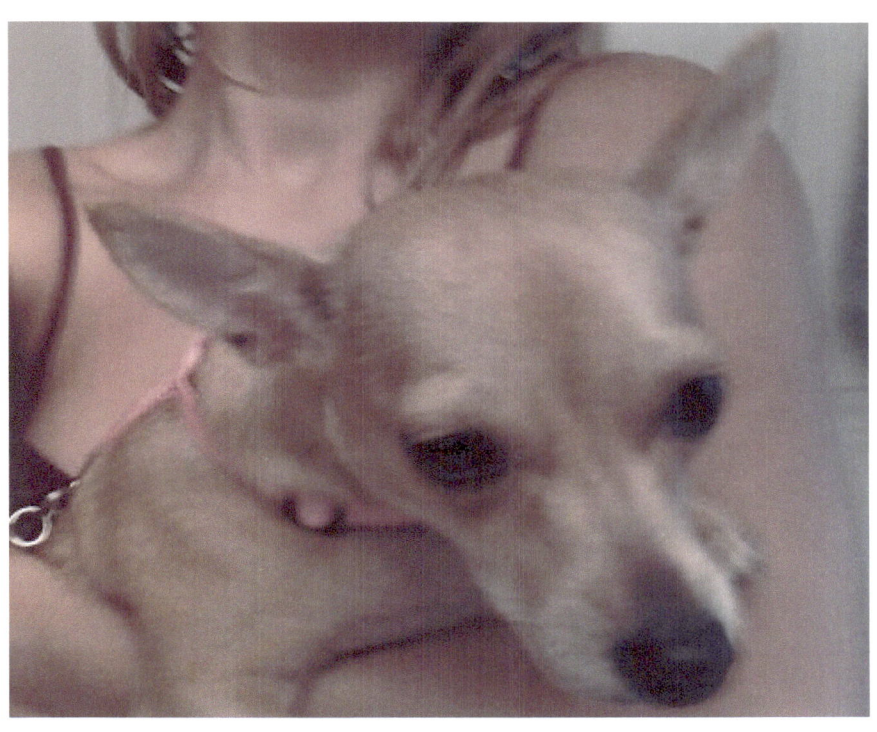

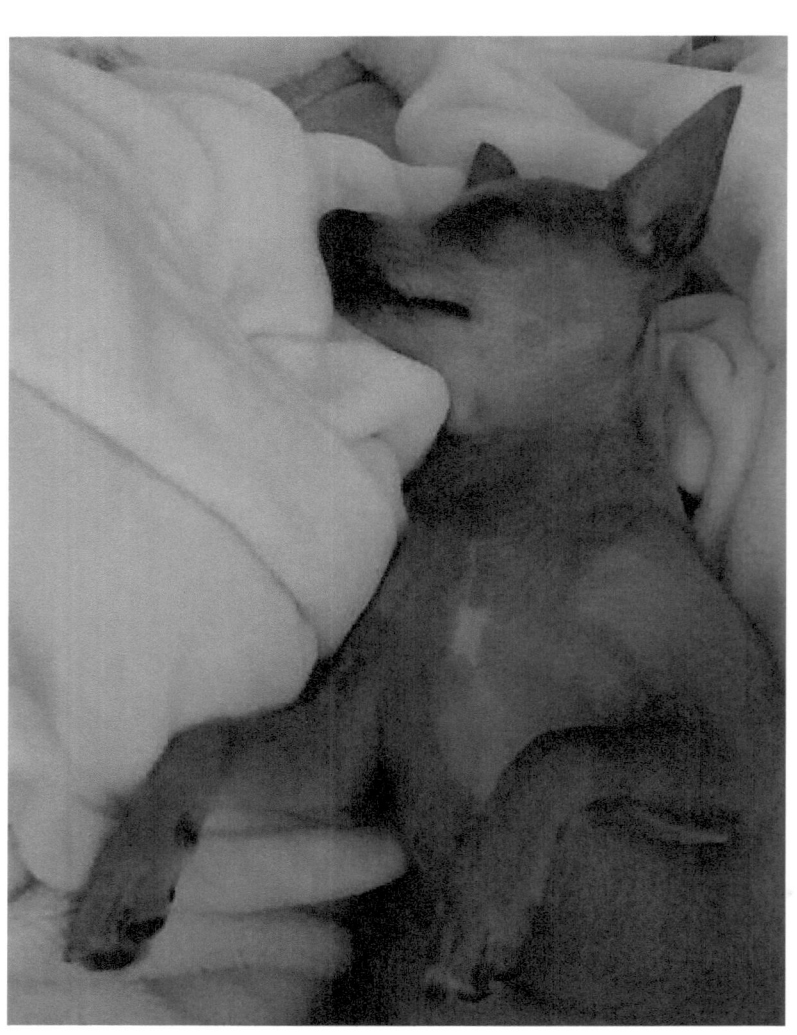

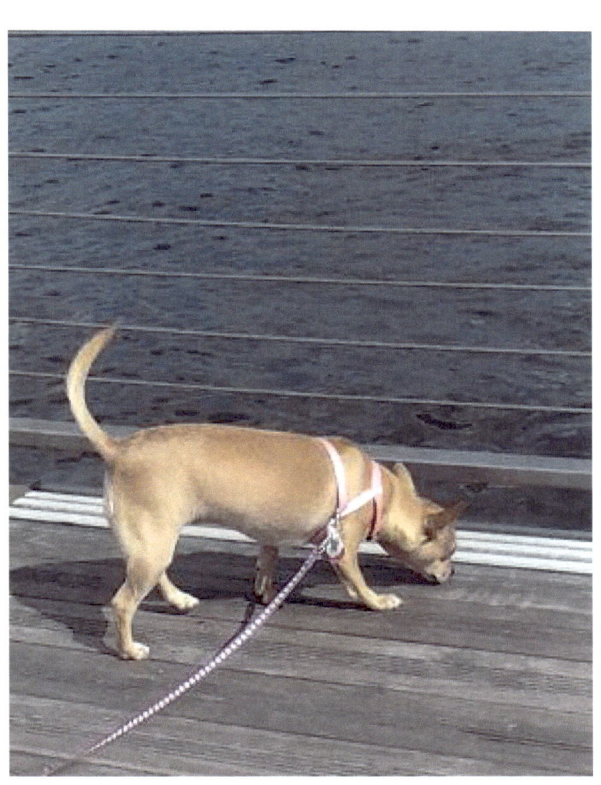

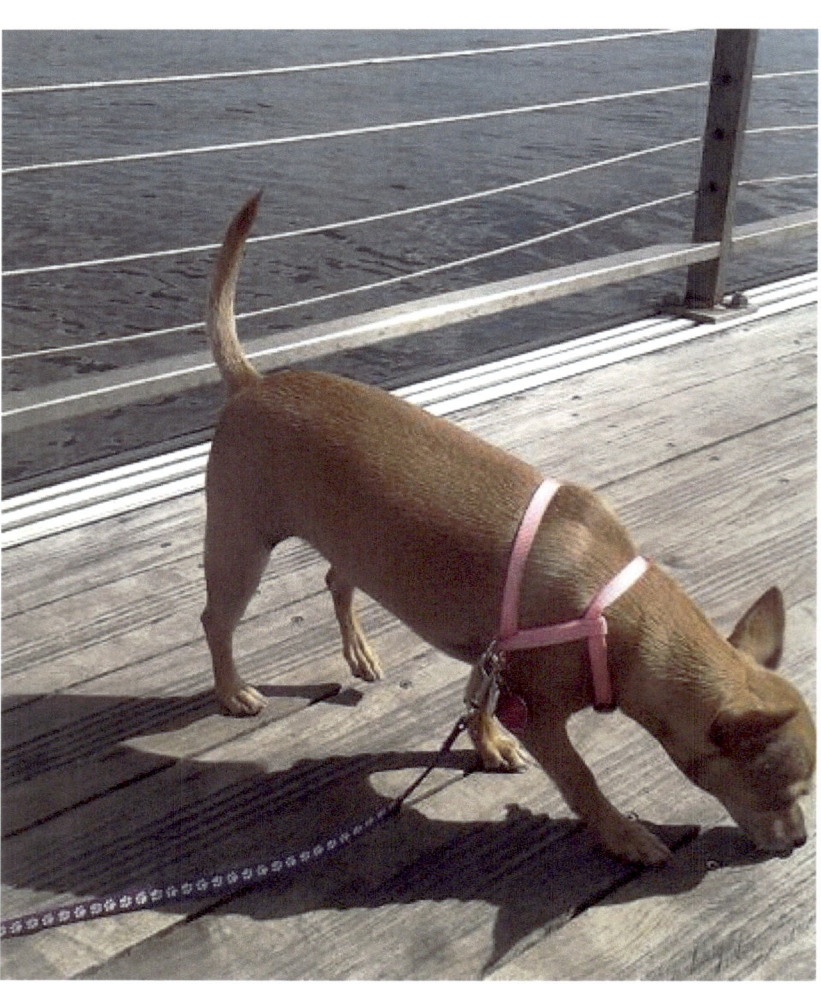

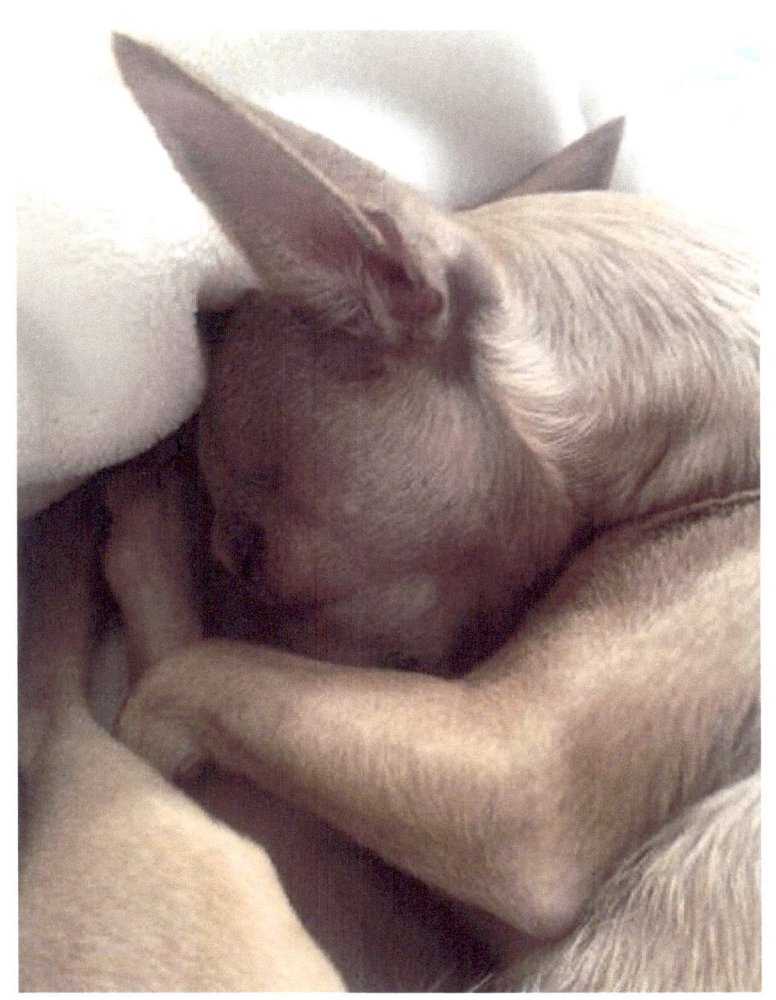

Nothing in the world, compares to the
love and companionship that of a dog.

My dearest Collette,
     you are my heart and soul.

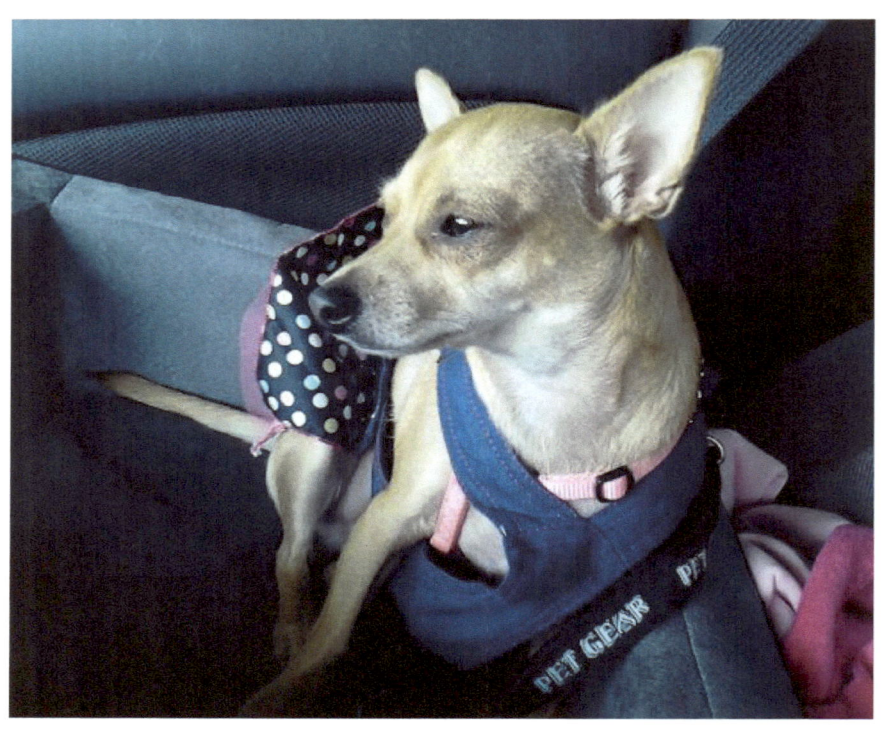

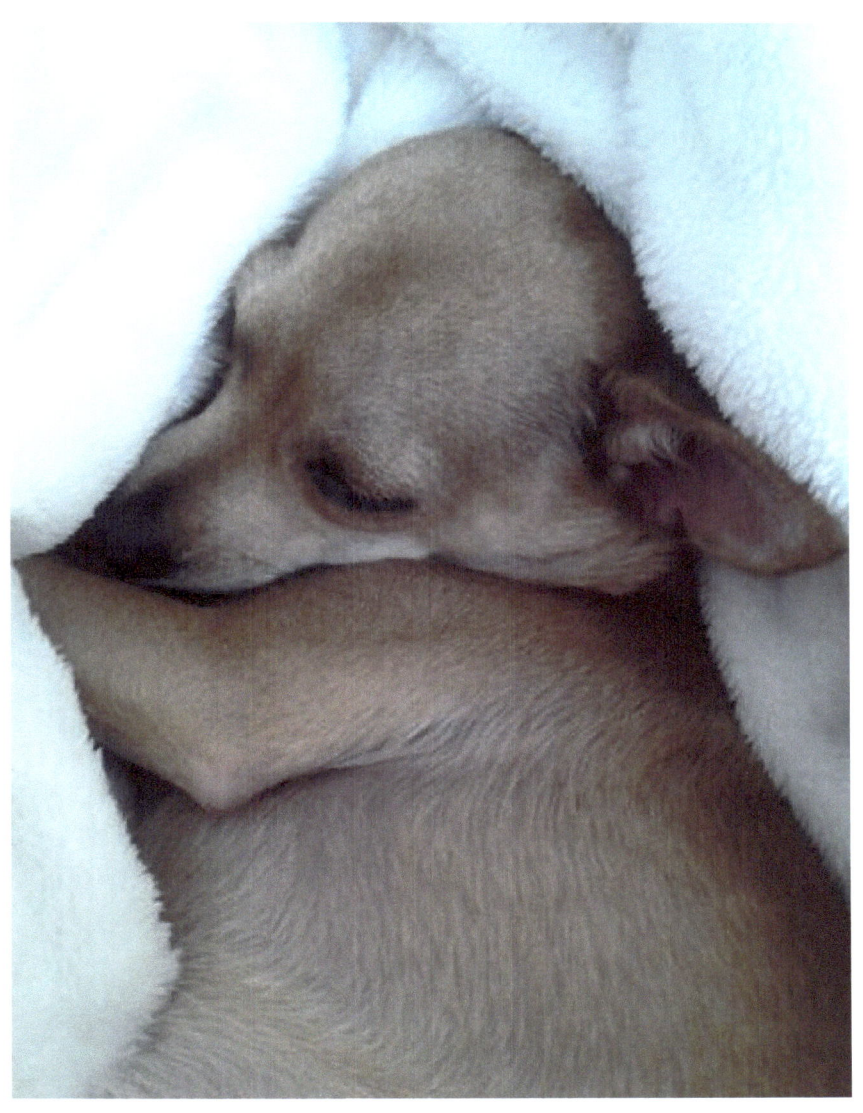

My cuddle bear

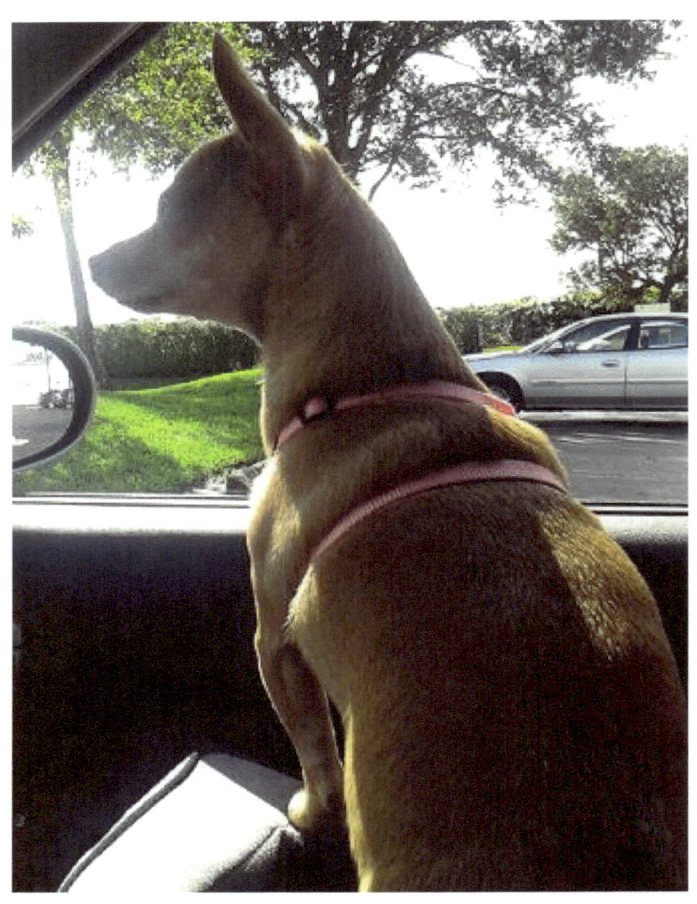

Always observing

In her car seat